BACKYARD BIRDS AND BIRD FEEDING

100 Things to Know

0 11557 03431 8

Backyard Birds and Bird Feeding

100 Things to Know

Sandy Allison, editor

STACKPOLE
BOOKS

Published by
STACKPOLE BOOKS
5067 Ritter Road
Mechanicsburg, PA 17055
www.stackpolebooks.com

Printed in the United States of America

10 9 8 7 6 5 4 3 2 1

First edition

Cover design by Wendy Reynolds
Cover photo © Getty Images

Library of Congress Cataloging-in-Publication Data

Backyard birds and bird feeding: 100 things to know / Sandy Allison, editor. — 1st ed.
    p. cm.
  ISBN-13: 978-0-8117-3431-8
  ISBN-10: 0-8117-3431-5
  1. Birds—Feeding and feeds. 2. Birds I. Allison, Sandy.

QL676.5.B194 2007
598—dc22

                                                                2007005315

CONTENTS

Feeders and Feeding

Feeders Are Valuable All Year Long

Many people consider autumn the best time of year to set up a bird feeder because birds are attracted to backyard food sources when the weather turns harsh. Birds will visit feeders in any season, however, so there's really no wrong time to start; and some bird lovers feed birds all year. In the fall, migrating birds fill up to prepare for long flights. In the winter, when natural food supplies are scarce, birds need feeders to help them survive in the cold. In the spring, as the weather gets warmer and birds prepare to nest, they visit feeders as they wait for natural foods to become abundant. In the summer, hummingbirds and orioles visit nectar feeders, and parents of various species bring their young to feed.

Those who don't feed the birds all year know it's important to at least keep feeders up and fully stocked through the early spring, when nesting and egg laying act as stressors and increase birds' calorie requirements. A good rule of thumb: Don't take a feeder down until the leaves are fully out on the trees.

A Good Breakfast Is Important

Birds awaken very early in the morning, usually before sunrise, and the first thing they do is look for food. To ensure that there is plenty of food for birds first thing in the morning, it's a good idea to fill your feeders in the evening. If many birds visit your feeders throughout the day, you might also want to be sure they don't go empty in the afternoon, as birds need to eat before they go to sleep.

It's also wise to stay aware of local events that could affect natural food sources. Feeder use may increase if nearby fields are eliminated because of development, for example, or if an ice storm locks away wild food. Do the birds a favor and keep your feeders full whenever weather conditions are bad.

Fat and Protein Are Good for Birds

Generally, backyard birds fall into four food preference groups: seed eaters, insect eaters, fruit and berry eaters, and nectar eaters. Seed eaters will eat a wide variety of commercial bird feeds. You can buy all one type of seed or mixes that contain several types. Bird feed is regulated by federal and state law that requires the listing of ingredients in the order of their percentage in the mix by weight. Each package must also carry a nutritional analysis of the contents; this is listed in terms of crude protein, fat, fiber, and moisture in the whole of the mix. In general, the higher the proportion of protein and fat, the better the seed mixture. Any seed you buy should be relatively dry—no more than thirteen percent moisture.

Black Oil Sunflower Seed Tops the List

Black oil sunflower seed is the most attractive food to the widest variety of seed-eating birds. Research at the Cornell Laboratory of Ornithology indicates that birds prefer black oil sunflower seed two to one over other sunflower seed varieties. The commercial black oil seed you buy should have been cleaned, recleaned, and de-sticked before it was packaged. Black-striped sunflower seed is attractive to larger seed-eating birds such as cardinals and grosbeaks, but it's not nearly as popular to an assortment of birds as black oil seed is.

Different Birds Like Different Seeds

Other seeds in commercial mixes appeal to certain species. A popular seed for goldfinches, redpolls, and pine siskins is niger seed, sometimes spelled *nyjer* and also known as thistle. It's a tiny, thin, black seed usually imported from Ethiopia or India and sterilized before it's sold in the United States.

Safflower seed is often touted as being squirrel-proof (although this claim is doubtful). Nevertheless, cardinals, titmice, and doves readily eat the pure-white seed, which is grown in the Midwest and California. Such seed is sometimes slightly discolored when the growing season is wet; the discoloration has no effect on safflower seed's popularity or nutritional value.

Tiny, round white proso millet is a common ingredient in seed mixes, although its appeal is generally limited to juncos, sparrows, and doves. Cracked corn is found in some mixes; cardinals and other ground feeders love it, but it often attracts grackles, which some consider a nuisance. Peanut hearts are included in some mixes, although they are not as appealing as split peanuts, which chickadees, titmice, and white-throated sparrows relish.

Not All Seeds Are Good Seeds

Commercial mixes with a high percentage of less-popular seeds should be avoided because uneaten seed spoils and fosters mold and fungi growth. Rapeseed is taken by some doves, finches, and juncos; but unless these species eat plenty, it will most likely go to waste. Golden millet and red millet are not nearly as popular as white proso millet and are likely to be ignored, as are flax and buckwheat. Canary seed, wheat, and oats are particularly popular with house sparrows and cowbirds, which most bird lovers don't see the need to feed. And while some birds will go for popped popcorn, it spoils very quickly, especially if it's damp. If you do offer popcorn, make sure it's not the microwaved, buttered, or flavored kind.

Niger Thistle Isn't Native Thistle

Even though imported niger seed (which has the scientific name *Guizotia abyssinica*) is commonly called thistle, it shouldn't be confused with the seed from thistle plants that are native to North America. Native thistle is of the genus *Cirsium*; and the most common is Canada thistle, which is a prevalent and familiar weed throughout the continent. Confusion about the names might come from the goldfinch's propensity to use fluffy *Cirsium* thistledown to line its nest. Goldfinches also eat the plant's tiny seeds. You can be sure that the thistle referred to in any commercial birdseed ingredient list, or that is to be used in "thistle feeders," is really niger.

Platform Feeders Are Most Effective

Because it offers easy access to a variety of seeds, a platform feeder—often just a shallow tray raised off the ground a few inches or several feet—is probably the most effective type of feeder. But as bird lovers soon learn, platform feeders can be too effective; birds, as well as squirrels and other mammals, can quickly deplete even the largest platform's food supply. If you set up a platform feeder, be prepared to refill it at least a couple of times a day.

The common hopper feeder, a platform feeder that includes some kind of box or housing that holds the seeds, releasing them onto the platform or tray a few at a time, is a good alternative. In fact, it's one of the most popular type of feeder available. Most hopper feeders can be hung or placed atop a pole. They can be filled with mixed seeds to attract an assortment of birds or with one kind of seed only.

Tubes Should Dispense One Type of Seed

Another common type of feeder is a tube feeder, which is usually made of plastic and has perches below openings that allow limited access to the seeds inside. One reason tube feeders are so appealing is that they mimic favorite wild food sources, such as the long stems of asters. The feeder's perches simulate limbs or branches, and the openings are like seedpods. Keep in mind that plants only produce one kind of seed, so a tube feeder shouldn't contain a mixture. If the holes are large enough, the best bet is to fill the feeder with black oil or striped sunflower seeds. Double-tube feeders feature two tubes in a wooden holder.

Special Tube Feeders Attract Finches

American goldfinches and other finches can be attracted to your yard with a type of tube feeder known as a finch feeder—it has tiny openings just large enough for very small seeds. Like any tube feeder, it should be filled with only one type of seed. Niger seeds or unshelled sunflower seeds work best for finches. Depending on where you live, finch feeders might also attract purple finches and Cassin's finches. They might even attract pine siskins, grosbeaks, crossbills, and redpolls during especially harsh winters when "irruptions" of these species come south from Canada.

Finch feeders also attract house finches, which some consider an unwelcome guest because they are so numerous and aggressive (house finches are native, but those in the eastern United States are the descendants of cage birds imported from California in the 1940s). Some finch feeders are designed to discourage house finches. One model is an "upside-down" feeder with the perches placed above the openings. Goldfinches don't mind hanging upside down to get food; house finches prefer to feed while standing upright. Another model has small perches that house finches have trouble using.

Exposed Feeders Are Often Ignored

If birds don't seem to visit a well-stocked feeder, it's rarely because there are no hungry birds in the area. It's often because the feeder is isolated with no safety cover nearby. Songbirds, like most wild creatures, are extraordinarily cautious. They will not fly out in the open if they sense that doing so might be dangerous. The most effective way to eliminate a bird's reluctance to stop at a feeder is to put it near a large shrub or bush or the branches of a tree—as close as five feet, if possible. That way, birds can make a quick and comfortable trip to feed and easily fly to safety if they sense a threat. As well, some birds, chickadees and titmice in particular, won't eat at a feeder at all; they'll grab a seed and fly away to eat it in safety. If you can't move the feeder, then putting a bush nearby—even a potted one or a discarded Christmas tree—will make the feeder much more enticing.

Simple Steps Keep Feeders Disease Free

While no disease is commonly spread through bird feeding alone, there are some bird diseases that can be spread by bad seed or unsanitary conditions. Aflatoxins, which are widespread in nature, can grow in birdseed and be spread to birds. Aspergillosis can grow in decaying vegetable matter and moldy birdseed. Avian pox can affect birds, causing eye damage and wartlike growths. Conjunctivitis, an eye disease, can affect house finches and goldfinches and is spread through flocks. Salmonella and trichomoniasis can also sicken backyard birds.

The best way to avoid spreading disease is to take a few simple precautions. Rake up shells and wasted seeds frequently and dispose of them, preferably in compost bins that are screened to keep out birds. Make sure feeders provide drainage so seeds dry quickly after a rain. If seeds are sprouting in a platform feeder, clean it out and add drain holes. Regularly clean feeders with a solution of one part household bleach to nine parts water and allow them to dry thoroughly before refilling.

Smart Storage Protects Birdseed

Store birdseed in a dry place to prevent fungus and other disease organisms from contaminating the supply. Never use old or moldy seed. Look for seed that has been screened for aflatoxin—not all of it has, and birds can't detect the toxin in food. Don't buy corn in nonbreathable bags; aflatoxin can grow in damp corn. If you feed birds whole peanuts, make sure they are fit for human consumption. If you notice sick or infected birds gathering at your feeder, take it down right away and clean it or get rid of it and replace your stock of seed.

Homegrown Seeds Work Just as Well

Raising seeds yourself is simple, inexpensive, and a great way to reduce your bird-food budget. All you need is a small patch of fertile ground that receives full sunlight and water for irrigation. The obvious choice for a bird-food garden is sunflowers. They thrive in full sun, and just a few heads yield a surprising amount of seed. Though sunflower seeds from packaged commercial food will work, it's best to use fresh seeds from a garden center to sow a new crop.

To maximize sunflower seed production in a small space, try the Mammoth Russian variety. These huge flower heads can produce hundreds, even thousands, of seeds. Birds will flock to the standing crop, or you can cut the ripe heads in the fall and store them for later use.

Another group of seeds that can be homegrown is often overlooked because we grow these plants for food and typically throw away the seeds. Watermelons, cantaloupes, pumpkins, and squashes are filled with seeds that many birds love. When you eat these garden foods, save the seeds. Just rinse, dry, and store them in a container as you would any other seed. Cardinals, chickadees, titmice, nuthatches, and woodpeckers relish these seeds, which are now showing up in expensive commercial mixes.

Uncooked Rice Won't Hurt Birds

It's a widely held belief that uncooked rice should not be offered to birds because it will swell in their stomachs and kill them if they eat it. This is the reason packets of birdseed instead of rice are tossed at the bride and groom after some weddings. The Cornell Laboratory of Ornithology notes, however, that birds suffer no ill effects from eating uncooked rice. In fact, bobolinks, nicknamed "rice birds," eat rice in the wild all the time. Of course, there's nothing wrong with throwing birdseed after weddings—birds will readily eat it, too.

Suet for Birds Is Easy to Make

Suet put out in specially made suet cage feeders or bags attracts a host of insect eaters. Although commercially prepared suet is widely available, homemade suet cakes are inexpensive and easy to make. Another big plus is the ability to control the ingredients. Many grocery stores and butcher shops sell suet for just pennies a pound. You can also collect your own, trimming fat from the cuts of meat you buy. Bag this and store it in the freezer until you have several pounds. To make suet more appealing to a greater variety of birds, add cornmeal, oatmeal, sunflower seeds, peanuts, almonds, walnuts, bacon grease, or peanut butter. Raisins, currants, or chopped fruit will attract bluebirds, orioles, and catbirds. Vegetable shortening makes a fine suet substitute. Simply smear a few spoonfuls of an inexpensive brand on the trunk of a tree.

A good recipe for homemade suet cakes is to melt one cup of lard and one cup of chunky peanut butter, combine, then stir in two cups of quick-cook oats, one cup of flour, and a third of a cup of sugar. Pour the mixture into square freezer containers about an inch and a half thick. Cool, cut into cakes, and serve to the birds. Keep the rest in the freezer.

The downside to suet is that it spoils quickly in hot weather. Birds may still eat it, but it can be a smelly mess. Many bird lovers limit suet feeding to the colder months, when birds need high-fat food the most.

Hummingbirds Have a "Sweet Beak"

Hummingbirds are a favorite backyard visitor, and they are often attracted to hummingbird feeders, which dispense food via sipping spouts. Sugar water is standard hummingbird fare, and it's easy to make. Under normal circumstances, one quarter to one third of a cup of white sugar to one cup water is the optimal mixture. Natural nectars vary in sugar content, and these concentrations are within normal ranges. A slightly stronger concentration might be beneficial during cold or rainy periods, when the birds need more energy. A weaker concentration is recommended during drought conditions.

Honey should never be substituted for sugar. Fungi and bacteria grow far more readily in honey than in processed sugar. During warm weather, sugar water will spoil, too, however; or it will ferment and could damage the livers of the birds that drink it. Hummingbird feeder water should be changed frequently, at least every two or three days, more often during especially hot weather. It's wise to place feeders in shady, cooler locations, if possible.

Coloring the sugar water is not necessary. It's the color and design of the feeder that attract hummingbirds, not the color of the nectar. Plain sugar is cheaper and probably more healthful for birds than are commercial hummingbird mixtures. If the feeder perches are big enough, orioles might drink from a hummingbird feeder, as might downy or acorn woodpeckers. Other species, including some warblers, have been known to develop a sweet beak, too.

Sipping While Seated Suits Hummingbirds

Many people mistakenly believe that perches on a hummingbird feeder are harmful to the birds. Apparently, at some point in time, hummingbirds around someone's feeder seemed to be dazed, and the story spread that the birds had taken a long sip of cold nectar in the morning while perched and were shocked by the frigid drink into a torporlike trance. Removing the perches, it was reasoned, would force the birds to fly while sipping, thus generating heat. *Bird Watcher's Digest* reports that there is no evidence that perches have ever caused hummingbirds any harm. In fact, the perches-are-bad story was listed as one of the magazine's "top ten feeder myths."

Hummingbirds Need Nectar

Nectar is secreted by glands located on many of a flower's interior surfaces. A hummingbird laps flower nectar using its tongue, which is long and forked like a snake's. The tongue has tiny tube-like structures on its surface that wick up nectar and a thin membrane along its edges that acts as a nectar scoop. The tongue is controlled by a large coil of muscle that occupies much of a hummingbird's skull. The bird can lap at a rate of fifteen times per second. The hummingbird's distinctive bill, which is somewhat soft and easily damaged, acts as the tongue's sheath.

Planting nectar-producing flowers is a great way to attract hummingbirds. Beach rosemary, yellow jessamine, Japanese honeysuckle, lyre-leaf sage, red buckeye, coral honeysuckle, wild azalea, fire pink, Indian pink, scarlet gilia, bee balm, and jewelweed are a few hummingbird favorites. Hummingbirds will also take sap from the tree-trunk wells drilled by yellow-bellied sapsuckers.

Hummingbirds Like Bugs Best

Although nectar is an important part of a hummingbird's diet, the birds are mainly insect eaters. They snatch bugs in midair, glean them from branches and stems, take them from flowers, even grab them off the ground. During peak nesting and breeding months, the hummingbird's diet is mainly insects—the birds may virtually disappear from feeding sites at this time.

Insects Play a Vital Role

Bird lovers shouldn't be too quick to reach for the spray can when they see an insect infestation in their yards or gardens. Such infestations are often natural and occur on healthy plants that can usually handle a few bugs or on unhealthy plants that should be thinned out anyhow. They also can be a banquet for birds. (A bird lover in Virginia reports growing perennial pea vines that invariably grow weak near the end of the summer. When they do, the shriveled leaves attract aphids, as well as a colorful flock of hungry goldfinches that keep the bugs in check, even as the bugs keep the vines in check.) Caterpillars, because they visibly damage green leaves, are an especially bothersome pest to some gardeners. But these creatures provide a high-energy feast for birds, and eliminating them completely from a garden will inevitably eliminate some visiting birds as well.

Insects, although they are disliked by many, play a vital role in the natural world. An occasional infestation is part of a balanced ecosystem. Smart gardeners realize this; and they also know that if infestations happen all the time, it's a good sign that something in the landscape is out of whack.

Bird Food Can Be Worms

Bluebirds and other insect eaters don't usually visit feeders, but they can sometimes be attracted if you offer them mealworms, which are the larvae of darkling beetles. Mealworms can be found in pet shops or bait stores or ordered in quantity online. To store mealworms, put them in a plastic bucket containing dry oatmeal or cornflakes or any other dry grain product. Add a few pieces of raw potato, carrot, or apple for moisture. Don't freeze the worms; they get mushy when thawed.

To serve mealworms, put live ones in a shallow bowl or on a platform feeder. It might take a little time for bluebirds to discover the food; but once they do, they'll devour it, as will catbirds, warblers, tanagers, and woodpeckers. Because mealworms can be expensive, supplementing them with commercial "insect" suet is a good idea.

Another way to attract insect-eating birds to the yard is to attract insects with a sweet slurry you can make yourself. Start with sugar water mixed up for hummingbirds; add pancake syrup and juice from canned fruits and a little ripe banana. Don't use honey. Serve in a small container, or simply wipe it on a tree trunk.

Bread Isn't Good for Birds

There's no doubt birds will eat bits of stale bread, but it's not the most beneficial food you can offer. Bread doesn't provide much nutritional value; in cold weather, birds need high-fat and protein-rich foods. Bread also tends to attract starlings, grackles, and crows. If you choose to offer bread, do so sparingly; try to offer quality seeds and suet as well. And avoid putting any food for ground feeders in the same spot day after day. Doing so increases the risk of disease. Move ground food around—hungry birds are sure to find it.

Use Care When Offering Fruit or Jelly

Some birds that never visit feeders for seed will come for fruit. Orioles, catbirds, woodpeckers, robins, and tanagers are all attracted to fruit in the spring. Grapes, apples, currants, bananas, raisins, and oranges are all good offerings. Don't leave out more fruit than the birds can eat in a couple of days, however, as it may rot or get moldy. Some feeders are specially made to hold half sections of larger fruits.

Jelly is also a popular food for fruit eaters, although it's not suitable for fledglings because they need food that's richer in protein. If a parent and chicks are visiting the feeder, it's time to remove the jelly. To serve jelly, spoon it into jar tops or other small containers. Don't offer more than a spoonful or two; birds can get mired in larger amounts. If your fruit or jelly attracts ants or flying bugs, so much the better. Birds will snatch these up, too.

Birds Need Calcium and Grit

Because they lay eggs, birds have very high calcium requirements. In places where acid rain has leached calcium from the soil, birds often suffer from a lack of needed minerals. As well, seed-eating birds require grit in their gizzards to help them grind their food. Providing eggshells from the kitchen and crushed oyster shells purchased from a pet shop can provide birds with both of these necessities.

Because the risk of salmonella is high in raw eggs, all eggshells (except those that have been hard-boiled) should be baked for twenty minutes at 250 degrees Fahrenheit before they are given to birds. Allow the shells to cool, then crush them into pieces at least as small as dimes. Offer them in a dish, on the ground, or on a low platform feeder, separate from seed feeders. A wide variety of birds have been observed picking up eggshells, including chickadees, tanagers, thrushes, warblers, jays, blackbirds, quail, and swallows.

A No-Salt Diet Is Best

Although birds need calcium, their salt requirements are minimal. Studies show that while grosbeaks, crossbills, and siskins in particular need a little salt in their diets, they usually get all they need from their natural foods or perhaps by drinking from tidal pools. Most birds do not want or need salt. Some observers report seeing birds feeding along the sides of snowy roads, supposedly looking for road salt. They were more likely looking for grit, or for food that was uncovered by a snowplow.

Squirrels Are Here to Stay

As soon as you put out any type of bird feeder anywhere in the country, you will almost certainly attract squirrels—and it's probably unrealistic to expect that any feeder will be squirrel-proof, no matter what its manufacturer claims. The best you can hope for is that getting food will be so difficult for squirrels that they won't eat too much. Entire books have been written on ways to outwit squirrels, although no one has yet developed a foolproof system.

Many bird lovers believe baffles work best. These are usually broad metal discs placed below the feeder around a pole or above the feeder if it hangs. For a baffle to work well it must be more than five feet off the ground (squirrels can leap that high), and the feeder must be at least five feet away from anything that a squirrel can use as a launching pad.

Tube feeders surrounded by metal cages can also reduce the amount of seed a squirrel can reach, as long as the cage's holes are small enough. But squirrels will almost certainly cling to cage feeders and reach for whatever seed they can grab with their paws, which can be quite a bit.

A hopper feeder that automatically closes when something heavy sits on the perch can also reduce a squirrel's intake, although it will also deter heavy birds. Squirrels will cling to the roof or the sides of such a feeder and be able to reach at least some seed without causing the feeder to shut. Some people grease the feeder pole or use a squirrel-shocking system, but these methods are not recommended. The upshot is that many feeder deterrents will work to some degree. But will they keep squirrels from eating any seed at all? Most likely not.

City Dwellers Must Not Feed Rats

Some bird lovers accept that squirrels will be backyard visitors and so offer them foods they love—peanuts and corn in particular—in special "squirrel feeders" placed away from bird feeders. These feeders can attract other mammals, however, including mice, raccoons, deer, even bears; so they must be monitored closely and taken down if problems develop. City dwellers should never feed squirrels if they can help it (or pigeons and ducks either, for that matter). Doing so will almost certainly help the local rat population. To avoid this, some cities have taken to educating their citizens with "Feed a Pigeon, Breed a Rat" reminders.

Wild Animals Should Remain Wild

It's a bad idea to try to make pets out of wild animals. It's fine to feed birds, because this does not cause them to change their behavior toward humans—birds will continue to fly away whenever a person comes too near. Wild mammals that come to associate humans with food, however, can be very dangerous to both people and themselves. Never hand-feed wild mammals. You risk being bitten, and you are putting the animals at risk. Such animals become beggars, approaching humans for handouts; because to a wild mammal, all humans are the same. And when a wild animal approaches for no apparent reason, many people are justifiably frightened. A person who encounters a seemingly unafraid animal might kill it or report it to law enforcement officials—who might kill it as well, believing it to be rabid.

Do not try to befriend wild mammals by throwing food out when they are within sight, and don't sweet-talk them as you would a pet. Does this mean you should not make any food available to wild mammals? No, it does not. The point is that mammals should not get the idea that you are putting out food especially for them.

Fake Owls Don't Work

Artificial owls can be a common sight on backyard decks and fence posts, especially in coastal areas where gulls are numerous. Do these fake owls do anything to frighten off gulls, crows, and other bothersome species? Most experts say no. They agree that a decoy might deter some birds from approaching for a few days, but after that, birds become used to the silent, unmoving intruder and pay it no mind.

Avian Flu Viruses Shouldn't Deter Birding

Avian influenza viruses have circulated in bird populations for centuries, and most pose no threat to birds or humans. One particular avian flu virus, H5N1, has caused much concern in recent years. This highly pathogenic virus has been detected in a handful of bird species, the majority of which are domestic poultry, and has killed several hundred people worldwide. Nearly all cases of human illness from H5N1 involved people who came in close contact with diseased poultry or tainted poultry products. No person in the United States has ever been sickened by the H5N1 virus. The only known cases of wild birds transmitting H5N1 to humans occurred in Azerbaijan.

Citing these facts, the Cornell Laboratory of Ornithology says that it is safe to feed birds and monitor nest boxes. Of course, it's always advisable to wash your hands thoroughly with soap and water after handling feeders, birdbaths, or nest boxes, and you should avoid touching dead birds or bird droppings with your bare hands. But the chance of picking up any kind of flu virus from bird-feeding activities is almost nonexistent.

Some Move Far Away, Others Stay Close

Which birds show up at a feeder and when is determined in large part by when and how far the birds migrate. Bird lovers know that some species appear only in winter, some appear during fall or spring migrations, some appear only in summer, and some are around all year long.

Scientists divide birds that migrate into three groups. Complete migrants leave their breeding range during the nonbreeding season. Most make nests and lay eggs in northern temperate and arctic areas then migrate to their wintering grounds, which for North American birds includes South and Central America, the Caribbean basin, and the southernmost United States. Most warblers, hummingbirds, shorebirds, tanagers, vireos, orioles, flycatchers, and thrushes are complete migrants. Some of these species fly incredible distances between their breeding and nonbreeding grounds.

Partial migrants may or may not make a seasonal movement away from their breeding grounds; some individuals do, some don't. The result is an overlap within a species between the breeding and nonbreeding ranges. For example, the Bewick's wren is a year-round resident from southern Illinois to the Gulf coast. East of the Mississippi, its breeding range extends into Minnesota and Wisconsin; but it is absent from this part of its range in winter. Partial migrants move to take advantage of seasonally abundant foods. Partial migration is by far the most common type.

Some Make Occasional Migrations

A third type of migration involves irruptive migrants. The migration of irruptive species is not seasonally or geographically predictable. The birds may migrate one year, then stay put the next, and for many years after. The great gray owl is an irruptive migrant. These owls spend all year north of the United States—except every once in a while, when they migrate in great numbers to the northeastern states, to the delight of local birders.

Northern finches and crossbills are irruptive migrants as well. Every so often they visit feeders south of their usual range by the thousands. Scientists don't yet know exactly what triggers irruptive migration, but they believe the variability of the food supply plays a role.

Bird Feeding Doesn't Delay Migration

A common myth is that feeding wild birds will keep them from migrating at their normal times and so endanger them. Scientists tell us, however, that bird feeding is unlikely to cause the vast majority of birds to remain in a location longer than usual; although feeders do provide food for individuals whose migratory timing or route varies from the norm and injured birds that aren't capable of migration. Stray orioles, thrashers, and some others may remain at feeding stations well north of the species' typical range for an entire winter. In fact, many of the rarities found on Christmas Bird Counts are birds that remain farther north than their normal range and are regularly visiting feeders. But orioles, thrashers, hummingbirds, and most others time their migration for the weeks when natural food is most abundant rather than when food is starting to disappear. So food availability is not a deciding factor that keeps individual birds past their normal departure time, especially long-distance migrants.

Some hummingbirds that find themselves north of where they "belong" in early winter may take refuge at a feeding station, but without the feeder, they'll simply die unnoticed. Some birds that linger may be injured, but most birds overwintering north of their "typical" range simply represent a normal variation within the species.

Many short-distance migrants such as blackbirds, juncos, and native sparrows are wintering north of their historical winter ranges because of changes in agriculture, habitat, and climate. A few nonmigratory species such as cardinals, titmice, and red-bellied woodpeckers have been steadily extending their year-round ranges northward in recent decades. Bird feeding contributes to the survival of individuals, so it has certainly played a role in their gradual range expansion, but it hasn't been the only or even the primary factor.

Attractive
Backyard Features

Water Is a Bird Magnet

Birds use water from a number of sources for drinking and bathing. These sources may be as small as a puddle or as large as a lake. If you don't have a natural supply of water on your property, there are several simple and inexpensive ways to create a water source that will attract birds. Buy a commercial birdbath—there are a wide variety of birdbaths on the market today. Or place a shallow dish filled with water on a tree stump. Or create a small pool by using a preformed fiberglass shell or by digging a hole and lining it with a suitable rubberized or plastic liner. If you have the space and the money, hire professionals to create a pond.

Whatever water source you use, keep a few things in mind. The water source must be shallow—no more than two inches deep—in at least one area so birds can bathe (songbirds can't swim). A rough surface on the inside of the bath will help birds maintain their footing. The water should always be clean. Regular scrubbing with white vinegar is recommended for heavily used birdbaths. Try to place your birdbath in a shady area near bushes or under branches so bathing birds can quickly find shelter if they need to.

Birds are especially attracted to running water, so you might try hanging a dripping hose over a shallow dish, conserving water with the aid of a recirculating pump system—available at most garden centers.

Metal Might Be Best for Birdbaths

Birdbaths are usually made of concrete, plastic, or metal. Each material has its advantages and drawbacks. Concrete is sturdy and won't tip easily, but it's heavy, which makes moving it difficult. It also requires cleaning once a week during warm weather because algae grow easily on its surface. And concrete birdbaths can't be used in winter because the water might freeze in the surface's many pores, causing it to crack.

Plastic is easy to maneuver and doesn't require as much cleaning as concrete, but it degrades quickly in sunlight and is lightweight, making the bath susceptible to tipping. If a plastic pedestal is hollow and can be filled with sand or gravel, the birdbath will be sturdier. Metal might be the best material for a birdbath. It can be used year-round; it's lighter than concrete and can be easily moved; and it's usually more substantial than plastic. Metal doesn't seem to grow algae as easily as concrete, either, so it doesn't require as much scrubbing to keep it clean.

Winter Water Is Important

Birds need water all year long, even during winter. Without it, they will die. Bird lovers who provide drinking water for birds in the cold months will attract a variety of wintertime visitors— bluebirds, robins, cedar waxwings, and yellow-rumped warblers, as well as regulars such as titmice, chickadees, cardinals, juncos, and white-throated sparrows.

An efficient winter birdbath requires a heating element—a device to keep at least some of the water from freezing during even the coldest conditions. Electric submersible heaters work well; most are thermostatically controlled to click on at about forty degrees Fahrenheit. Look for one with an automatic shutoff feature that turns the heater off if the water is gone. Always use a heavy-duty, outdoor-rated extension cord.

If you live in a temperate climate, you can refill your birdbath with warm water on cold mornings as needed. In colder climates, however, this is probably not practical. Never use any kind of chemical to keep birdbath water unfrozen—you risk poisoning the birds if you do.

Birds Skip Cold Baths

During cold weather, birds seem to know not to bathe. They'll drink water in cold weather by perching on the rim of a birdbath to avoid getting their feathers wet. Because not much blood flows through their extremities, they lose very little heat through their seemingly naked and unprotected feet.

Grow Trees to Get Birds

To enjoy backyard birds for the next twenty or thirty years, consider planting a few trees. Properly chosen, trees will provide food, shelter, and nesting sites for decades. The best way to get started is to buy older, more mature trees at a reputable nursery. These can be expensive, but many bird lovers believe they are well worth the cost. Once established, a stand of trees will become a hub of backyard bird life.

Some of the best trees to cultivate in any part of the continent are oaks. Acorns are a favorite food of everything from nuthatches and jays to woodpeckers and game birds. In the Northeast, white, red, and black oaks are good choices. In the South and along the Pacific coast, plant live oaks. In the prairie states, post, blackjack, and bur oaks do well. Gambel's oaks are best for the western mountains and valleys.

In fact, virtually any nut- or fruit-bearing tree makes a terrific addition to a backyard bird sanctuary. Pecan, walnut, and beech trees attract the same species that enjoy acorns. Mulberries, cherries, plums, crab apples, and figs draw bluebirds, waxwings, catbirds, robins, thrashers, and tanagers. A nursery or garden center can provide planting tips and recommendations for your region.

Because many birds nest in shrubs, they can be important bird attractors as well. What shrubs you should plant is determined by where you live. The best for birds are shrubs that grow into dense thickets and offer protection from hawks, cats, and owls. Thorny species are better than thornless kinds. And no backyard bird habitat is complete without a few fruit-bearing shrubs.

Conifers Are a Year-Round Favorite

Conifers offer year-round cover and are a great part of any backyard bird habitat. Doves, jays, robins, mockingbirds, and chipping and lark sparrows all nest in pines and spruces in spring; during winter, many species roost amid the protective cover of evergreen conifer branches. And finches extract the seeds from the cones of pine, fir, and spruce trees.

Planting conifers has other benefits. A bank of conifers on the west or north side of a home protects the building from chilly prevailing winds and can reduce heating costs. It's a great investment that will attract birds and increase the value of the property.

Birds Love Thickets and Brush Piles

Throughout the cold months of the year, a variety of birds spend much of their time in thick tangles of briars, vines, and other such plants. Cardinals, juncos, goldfinches, and all sorts of native sparrows rest in these thickets during cold or inclement weather. Providing shelter and escape cover like this in your yard will make it much more attractive to birds.

For immediate results, build a brush pile. Collect large branches trimmed from trees. Lay them crosswise, in tic-tac-toe fashion, in a corner of your yard. You can add to the pile throughout the year—ideally, it should be around six feet by six feet and at least three feet tall. You might want to insert a sheet of plywood a few feet off the ground for extra weatherproofing. Another source of brush material is discarded Christmas trees. Neighbors might be happy to let you have theirs, and retailers sometimes give away unsold trees after the holidays. A used Christmas tree can be placed underneath a bird feeder; tie it down so it doesn't blow around on windy days, or tie several together.

A more long-term project is to plant dense deciduous thickets of roses, raspberries, blackberries, barberries, or honeysuckle. A few grape, trumpet creeper, or Virginia creeper vines nearby will grow through the thicket, making it even more impenetrable and attractive to birds.

Dead Trees Attract Live Birds

The remnants of a dead or dying tree, known as a snag, are vital to many birds in the wild. Woodpeckers excavate nest cavities in snags and tear the wood apart in search of insects that riddle the innards. Bluebirds, titmice, wrens, screech-owls, and kestrels nest in old woodpecker holes. Red-tailed hawks perch on the top of snags to scan for prey. Phoebes launch fly-catching attacks from limbs. Vultures roost on large snags, warming their bodies in the morning sun. Buntings, vireos, cardinals, and many other birds sing from snags to advertise and defend their territories.

Snags are so valuable to birds that many bird lovers avoid cutting them down. In fact, many people plant snags, so-called "ghost trees," to supplement natural ones. A planted snag can be smallish—six inches around and ten or so feet tall—or huge; some people plant twenty-foot-tall snags in concrete footings. The best snags have stout, horizontal branches that act as perches, and from which feeders can be hung.

Planting a snag is straightforward, although large ones can be difficult to maneuver, requiring a truck or tractor to haul. For bigger snags, dig a hole four to six feet deep and about eight inches wider than the diameter of the snag's base. Hoist the snag into place, brace it, and fill the hole with concrete. Make sure the snag is vertical before the concrete sets. Smaller snags can be planted in holes filled with dirt that's been stamped down firmly.

Woodpeckers Can Be Pests

Home owners with wooden houses know that woodpeckers, particularly acorn woodpeckers in the West, can do substantial damage. Homes with clapboard, board-and-batten, or tongue-

and-groove siding, especially if it is unpainted or dark stained, are most attractive to the birds.

Woodpeckers make large holes when testing sites for nest holes and small holes when drilling for insects. What can be done to prevent woodpecker damage? Trapping or shooting virtually never work, and sticky coatings are often unsightly and cruel.

Experts recommend that home owners repair every woodpecker hole as soon as they can, with aluminum flashing, if possible. If a nest is not established, holes should be plugged and otherwise covered. (If a nest is active, wait until the chicks fledge.) Lightweight nylon or plastic netting can be attached to overhanging eaves to cover the siding of a damaged building, although the netting should be at least three inches away from the siding to keep woodpeckers from reaching through it. If a home is infested with insects, including wasps or carpenter bees, hiring an exterminator to get rid of them will go a long way toward controlling damaging birds.

Dust Baths Help Birds Stay Clean

Many species of birds take dust baths—they flap and scratch in dusty or sandy areas to raise a cloud, even roll around in the dust. Ruffed grouse, bobwhites, pheasants, wild turkeys, robins, bluebirds, cardinals, mourning doves, and a variety of other birds engage in this unusual activity. Experts believe they do so to help clean and maintain their feathers when standing water is not available; a dust bath is almost always followed by a bout of preening. Dust baths might also help sooth irritation caused by molting or mites.

Creating a dust bath is one of the easiest backyard bird projects you can tackle. Select an open, flat area with full exposure to sunlight. This ensures that the bath will stay as dry as possible and minimizes the risk from stalking predators. A spot three by three feet is adequate. Remove the sod and add the dust—equal parts sand and topsoil. Rim the perimeter with landscape timbers, bricks, or flat rocks. After a day or two of sunshine, the dust bath will be ready for dirty birds.

Nest Builders Love Scraps

Putting out good nesting materials in mesh bags or clean suet cages or simply wedging them into tree bark or between branches is a great help to backyard birds during nesting season, in late winter and spring. Suitable material to offer birds includes cotton quilt batting, frayed binder twine or yarn, thin strips of natural fiber cloth rags, dog and cat hair, sheep wool and horsehair, milkweed down, small poultry or pillow feathers, alfalfa stems, dead leaves, dry grass, bark strips, and pine needles. Some species also make use of spiderwebs, mud, lichens, and snake skins for nest building.

Lint from the dryer should *not* be left out for birds. When lint gets wet and then dries, it often becomes brittle; nests containing it could fall apart. And never leave out strips or strings longer than a few inches; long pieces are a choking hazard. Natural fibers are preferable to synthetics.

Nest Boxes Can Benefit Birds Enormously

For many bird lovers, nothing beats peeking out a window on a spring morning, seeing a bird carrying nesting materials to a nest box, and knowing that if the box wasn't there, that bird might not have nested at all. When a local habitat provides adequate food and cover but insufficient nesting sites, artificial nest boxes can make an enormous difference to local bird populations. In some cases, nest boxes have helped whole species make a comeback.

Unfortunately, improperly designed or situated boxes can cause eggs or nestlings to die from excessive heat or cold or to drown. When boxes are not properly maintained, lethal parasites can flourish. And some boxes are open invitations to house sparrows and starlings, two species that threaten native bird populations and do not need housing subsidies. With a few precautions, however, providing and monitoring nest boxes can be a beneficial and rewarding activity.

All Boxes Have Basic Requirements

No matter what the design, all nest boxes have some basic requirements. They should be built of wood at least three-quarters of an inch thick, which helps insulate the interior. (Boxes made of recycled plastic or concrete also work but are more expensive.) Boxes should not be made of treated lumber or painted on the inside, although earth-toned paints, stains, or sealers on the outside are okay. Boxes should be assembled with galvanized screws or nails so the fastenings won't rust. The roof should extend beyond the front of the box by several inches to protect the inside from driving rain, and the floor should have several quarter-inch drain holes to prevent flooding. Ventilation holes near the top of the box help keep it cool during hot days.

Nest boxes should not have perches, since cavity nesters have strong feet and can easily climb on virtually any wooden surface. Perches only assist predators. Boxes should be able to be opened easily for periodic cleaning. Uncleaned boxes often attract mice, which quickly render the box unusable.

Proper Hole Size Is Crucial

One of the most important features of any nest box is the size of its hole. If you hope to attract a specific species, you should use a box with a hole that suits that bird. A smaller hole will exclude it; a larger hole will undoubtedly attract larger species and perhaps unwanted intruders. The exact specifications for hole sizes (and for the boxes themselves) are available from a number of resources: birding magazines and books or online. Hole-size requirements for some popular cavity-nesting species are given here.

Chickadees require holes that are between $1^1/_8$ and $1^1/_2$ inches in diameter (the smaller size will exclude almost every other species except house sparrows). Tufted titmice, white-breasted nuthatches, Carolina wrens, downy woodpeckers, and tree swallows need $1^1/_2$-inch holes. Red-bellied and red-headed woodpeckers need 2-inch holes—and all woodpeckers need a box that's filled with sawdust or wood chips. Purple martins need $2^1/_8$-inch holes. Northern flickers need $2^1/_2$-inch holes. Screech-owls and American kestrels need 3-inch holes.

Some Species Need Help to Escape

Most nest boxes do not need any sort of "escape ladder" inside for nestlings to use when they fledge. When they are ready to leave the nest, the majority of cavity-nesting species are well developed and can easily reach the hole. Boxes used by swallows and ducks are exceptions, however. Tree swallows in particular migrate north early in the spring and can be caught by a sudden cold snap that sends insect prey into hiding. During these periods, swallows often seek shelter in nest boxes until warmer weather returns. When it does, weakened swallows may be unable to leave the box unless a piece of hardware cloth or series of grooves have been added to the inside underneath the hole.

As well, boxes intended for cavity-nesting waterfowl—especially wood ducks—require an escape ladder so day-old hatchlings can climb out. Such species brood their young for only twenty-four hours before coaxing them out of the nest and leading them to water.

Bluebirders Recommend Two Box Designs

Two types of bluebird boxes in particular are recommended: the Peterson box and the North American Bluebird Society box. The Peterson box is narrower at its bottom ($2^3/4$ inches) than at its top ($10^1/4$ inches), which means less nesting material is required. It also has a unique entrance: Rather than a simple hole, the entrance is $2^1/4$ inches high and $1^3/8$ inches wide; it can be made by drilling two overlapping holes with a $1^3/8$-inch drill bit. Bluebirds like this entrance because they can enter and exit more easily and adults can lean in to feed nestlings without having to squeeze inside themselves.

The Peterson box features a sloping roof that extends a few inches beyond the front and sides. This makes it difficult for raccoons and cats to sit on the box and reach inside. As well, the roof is double layered, making the box well insulated. Its front swings open to allow easy cleaning. Peterson boxes are available at bird centers and online retailers. You can find plans online, too. The Bluebird Society box is easier to build than the Peterson box. It's a 4-inch wide by 4-inch deep rectangular box with an entrance hole that's $6^1/2$ inches from the bottom of the box. It has a sloping roof and one side that swings open to permit easy cleaning. Plans for building it are on the society's website.

Owls Nest in Neighborhood Boxes

Many bird lovers have luck attracting screech-owls to nest boxes in suburban neighborhoods. A screech-owl box should have an 8-by-8-inch base, 17-inch-high back, 15-inch-high front, and sides that slope forward at their tops. The roof should overhang the front by a few inches. A box front that swings open will make cleaning easier. The box's hole should be 3 inches in diameter and positioned 10 inches above the base.

Hang a screech-owl box below a good-sized limb on a tree growing in a somewhat open area. The box should be at least 10 feet off the ground and face north, if possible. Choose a tree with a trunk that's wider than the box. It's a good idea to put an inch or so of dry leaves or wood shavings inside the box; owls won't bring nesting materials. Most screech-owls are tolerant of human activity. They've been known to nest within 10 feet of an occupied house.

Windows Are a Danger

Each year, millions of birds are injured or killed when they fly into windows. The birds sometimes see their own reflection, which causes them to attack; or they simply don't know that glass is in their flight path. The best way to solve the collision problem is to break up a window's reflection. The simplest method of preventing territorial birds from seeing their own image in a window is to tape paper or cardboard over it on the outside and leave it in place during the nesting season. A product known as CollidEscape will both eliminate the reflection and allow you to see out.

To prevent birds from inadvertently flying into a window throughout the year, break up the reflection with decals, curtains, streamers, or other suitable objects. Such objects must be placed within a few inches of each other to be completely effective.

It's important to position feeders and birdbaths far enough away from windows so that birds flying away quickly are safe from harm. An alternative is to use a window feeder that's placed within a foot of a window. Birds that exit these can't pick up enough speed to do much damage if they hit the glass.

Decals Don't Need to Be Hawkish

Decals shaped like hawks or other birds of prey are sometimes sold as the ultimate solution to the window-strike problem. Such decals will deter birds from hitting windows if they're placed close enough to each other—but not because birds are afraid of the depicted predator. Hawk decals simply break up glass reflection the same way any other decal would.

Rehab Centers Will Assist Injured Birds

If you find an injured bird in your yard, you might want to take it to the nearest wildlife rehabilitation center for treatment. The best way to capture the bird is to toss a towel over it, then scoop it up and place it in a paper bag, which you can then roll closed. If the bird is larger than a sparrow, you might have to close the bag with paper clips. If it's a large bird, or one with a sharp bill or talons, it's best to wear heavy gloves when you hold the towel-wrapped creature. If possible, go directly to a rehab facility. The people there will take your name, the date, the place you found the bird, and what caused the bird's injuries (if you know). Such facilities don't charge a fee, even though they don't get government funding. They generally depend on contributions.

If the wing of an injured bird is dangling and the bird isn't struggling too much, you can try to gently set the wing against the bird's body as well matched to the other wing as possible. Roll a towel or a product known as Vet Wrap around the bird to hold the wing in place. Don't wrap too tightly, however, or you might cause the creature to suffocate.

Pesticides Are Still a Problem

Countless birds still die each year from contact with landscape and agricultural chemicals. Direct poisoning occurs when a bird eats a pesticide granule, mistaking it for seed or grit, or is sprayed. Indirect poisoning occurs when a bird eats a poisoned insect or other food item.

To address this problem, many bird lovers try to reduce their dependence on chemical fertilizers. They carefully evaluate the potential pest threat: Will the problem go away without intervention? Is the pest something that can be lived with? They physically remove pests by hand or use pest-specific traps. They interplant species that repel pests or increase the number of natural insect predators—lacewings, ladybird beetles, toads, and, of course, birds—on their properties.

They use leaf and compost mulches, which can work as well as fertilizers to add nutrients to the soil and are usually much cheaper. If they decide to use chemicals, they use only ones made from naturally derived compounds, such as insecticide soaps. And since a lawn usually requires an enormous amount of pesticides and fertilizers, they reduce the amount of yard space given over to lawn, which greatly reduces the need for chemical use.

Indoors Is the Place for Cats

Of the seventy-eight million pet cats in the United States, more than half are allowed to go outside. The number of wild birds these roaming cats kill is difficult to calculate, although a few researchers have tried. One University of Wisconsin ornithologist estimates that seven million birds are killed by cats each year in his state alone. The American Bird Conservancy puts a country-wide estimate at hundreds of millions of birds killed a year.

Cats are predators by nature. But unlike foxes, coyotes, hawks, owls, and other bird-eating predators, we subsidize cats, providing them with food and shelter and caring for them when they are ill. On a single suburban block, three or four cats might thrive, whereas a family of foxes would require far more space and would either move or die out when they depleted their prey. Even the most well-fed cats have a natural instinct to chase and toy with birds and other small creatures; as a result, they will kill birds they have no intention of eating.

Cats let outdoors are themselves at risk. They can be hit by cars and injured in fights. They can be killed by dogs, foxes, hawks, and owls. In fact, cats allowed to roam outdoors have an average life span of around four years, compared with an average of some fifteen years for indoors-only cats.

Gardens Are Good for You

The National Federation of Garden Clubs is making a nationwide effort to add gardens to hospitals, nursing homes, assisted-living complexes, and hospices for the benefit of residents and visitors alike. It's not so surprising that such clubs would take an interest in creating these "healing gardens" since gardeners love to garden. What is more significant is that gardeners seem to be intuitively aware of how restorative the natural world can be to a person's state of mind.

Scientific studies are not required to prove the necessity of interacting with nature, at least on some level. Such studies, however, have shown that nature can have a powerful role in the physical healing process, especially in tension-filled environments such as hospitals. Research indicates that hospital patients who look out on a natural setting recovered more quickly than those who look out onto a brick wall. The theory is that a patient who is able to view trees and flowers in a gardenlike setting, especially one that includes birds and other wildlife, experiences a reduction in stress that promotes good health.

Backyard Visitors

Cardinals Are New to the North

Cardinals have dramatically expanded their original southern U.S. range northward during this past century, a trend that continues today. Cardinals began their northward expansion up the Mississippi River valley late in the nineteenth century. Appearing first as casual visitors in the North, they rapidly increased their presence in northern states throughout the 1900s.

Reasons for their successful northward expansion remain speculative. Frequently suggested possibilities are the increase of edge habitats (where wooded areas meet clearings), a period of mild winters during the early 1900s, and a more recent global warming trend. Much of the cardinal's range expansion has apparently occurred in winter, as the birds gravitated toward backyard feeders and fruit-rich swamps, thus establishing a foundation for local populations. Despite their southern origins, cardinals seem to suffer few lethal effects from cold weather.

Cardinals at first probably preferred forest openings. Today, just about any thicket vegetation, wet or dry, in forest or suburban yard, may host cardinals. Isolated patches of dense shrubbery seem to be the vital element, conditions ideally met in many residential areas, as well as along roadsides and in overgrown fields.

Hypothermia Helps Chickadees

The tiny black-capped chickadee weighs less than half an ounce, yet it can live through even the coldest and snowiest winter. How can such a small creature survive harsh conditions? On cold winter nights, chickadees go into regulated hypothermia, actually lowering their body temperature, in a controlled manner, down to about twelve to fifteen degrees Fahrenheit below their normal daytime temperature. This adaptation allows them to save enormous amounts of energy. When the outside temperature is at the freezing point, hypothermia reduces a chickadee's hourly metabolic expenditure by almost twenty-five percent, and as the outside temperature gets even lower, the energy savings increase.

Chickadees lower their body temperatures by reducing the amount of shivering they do. Shivering generates heat through muscular work; thus when a chickadee gradually reduces its shivering, its body temperature will fall. Chickadees never let their temperature get low enough to affect their ability to escape danger, however. Even when they are in hypothermia, they can still fly.

A few other adaptations help the black-capped chickadee survive the cold. Fluffing its feathers, foraging during lower light levels in the winter than in the summer, molting just before winter sets in, and feathers that cover its nostrils all work in the bird's favor.

Blackcaps and Carolinas Are Near Look-Alikes

The easiest way to distinguish a black-capped chickadee from its near look-alike, the Carolina chickadee, is to check the ranges of the two species. Black-capped chickadees spend all year in the northern half of the country and across Canada. Carolina chickadees live in the east-central and southeastern United States. The birds' ranges overlap only slightly—and it's in these regions that a careful look is needed to positively identify a chickadee at a feeder.

The black-capped chickadee's wing coverts, the short feathers on the "shoulders" of the wings, are broadly edged with white. The Carolina chickadee has less white on its wings, especially on the wing coverts. As well, the lower edge of the black bib on the black-capped chickadee tends to be uneven, sometimes having an almost scaled appearance. The division between the black bib and pale underparts on a Carolina chickadee is usually a neat, straight line. The whistled songs of the two species are different, too. The black-capped chickadee's song is a relatively simple two- or three-note *fee-bee* or *fee-beeyee*, whereas the typical Carolina chickadee song has four notes: *fee-bee fee-bay*.

The Snow Bird Is the Most Common

The dark-eyed junco is the familiar "snow bird" that shows up at feeders during winter throughout most of the country. The Cornell Laboratory of Ornithology's Project FeederWatch often lists the junco as the most common feeder bird in the United States, except in the southeast and deep south. Readily identifiable by its slate-gray upperparts, white underbelly, and pale bill, the junco is primarily a ground feeder. It picks up seeds that have fallen from feeders and scratches in leaf litter for food.

The several forms of dark-eyed juncos, which live in different parts of the country, were once considered separate species. Bird lovers who keep records often notice that the first juncos appear in their yards at around the same time each year—for some, it means winter is officially under way. By the time the weather turns warm, snow birds are gone. They spend spring and summer in northern Canada, although a few stay around all year in mountainous regions farther south.

Titmice Go from Loud to Silent

Few birds display such abruptly contrasting styles of behavior in a breeding season as does the tufted titmouse, a small, gray bird with a tufted crest, black forehead patch, and rusty flanks. By early spring, titmice have dispersed from their winter flocks into solitary wanderers and pairs. Territorial skirmishes and the incessant singing of males—most typically a loud, clear *peter peter peter*—mark this period. But as nesting commences in April and May, the birds fall silent and become difficult to detect. Titmice in the southern part of their range often breed twice, and the first fledglings help feed the second brood.

Titmice become most visible again in the winter, gathering in small family flocks and regularly visiting backyard feeders. They sometimes join mixed flocks of chickadees, downy woodpeckers, nuthatches, and kinglets. As territorial impulses quicken in late winter, yearling birds finally disperse to find their own places in the world; and the ringing songs start up again. In many places, titmice are the first vocal songbirds of the year.

Robins Are Adaptable Generalists

One of the most common residents around human dwellings, the American robin is a true yard bird. Its characteristic hop-and-stop gait in the grass, head cocking, and sudden thrust for an earthworm are familiar sights. Robins are true habitat generalists, able to occupy almost any land area that provides enough food, which is mainly fruits and berries (and worms during the breeding season). When building nests and raising young, robins often favor artificial parklands so prevalent in shady suburbs. Away from town, they frequent orchards, forest edges, and lake and stream margins. Unless severe weather forces them to move, wintering flocks favor swampy areas for feeding and roosting. The first robins of spring may actually have been residing in nearby wetlands all winter and are simply shifting habitat.

The robin's adaptability to human environs gives it a competitive edge over many other birds, although wintering robins must compete with other fruit eaters, including mockingbirds, cedar waxwings, and starlings. Their adaptability has made robins far more abundant today than in presettlement times; Native Americans and pioneers probably saw them rarely. They thrive today even though the widespread use of DDT in the 1950s and 1960s poisoned their spring food supply, causing robin populations to plummet. When DDT use was banned in this country, robin numbers rebounded quickly.

Robins Find Worms by Sight

After years of study, scientists have determined that robins locate earthworms primarily by sight, not by sound. The birds can detect the slightest movements, undiscernible to our eyes, of a worm in its near-surface burrow. Wet lawns attract robins because saturated soil drives worms to the surface for air.

"Lost" Fledglings Should Be Left Alone

If you find a baby bird that seems to have been abandoned, look carefully to see if its eyes are open and it's completely feathered.

If it is, the bird might be a fledgling that's been left on its own for a short time by its parents, who will probably soon return. In fact, they might be nearby, making noise. Fledglings look helpless, and they might not be able to fly; but they should be left alone.

If a baby bird is without feathers and obviously very young, it might have fallen from its nest. Try to find the nest and put back the baby. Handle the bird gently. Don't worry that its parents will reject it if it's been touched by a human—they won't. If you notice that a nest has fallen or blown down, try to replace it if you can. If you need to, put the nest in a suitable open container, such as a small plastic food tub, and nail the container to the place where you think the nest might have been. As a last resort, call a wildlife rehabilitator and ask for advice.

The Mockingbird's Repertoire Is Limitless

Ornithologist Frank Chapman called the northern mockingbird our "national songbird." One of the most accomplished vocal mimics in the bird world, the mockingbird advertises its presence loudly and incessantly, often from a conspicuous perch. Its song consists of multiple plagiarism, bits and pieces lifted from the repertoires of almost any other bird it has heard, plus frog croaks, dog barks, cat meows, gate squeaks, tire squeals, and so on. (One Indian tale, however, reverses the sequence: It says that the mockingbird taught all the other birds to sing, so they are the plagiarists.)

In any case, no two northern mockingbirds ever sing exactly alike. A single song bout may last up to ten minutes, a medley that itself may differ from the bird's past performances, or its next ones. It may repeat particular notes a dozen times before switching to another arrangement. Some male mockingbirds "have repertoires in excess of two hundred songs," according to one researcher, "the acoustic equivalent of a peacock's tail." In fact, the repertoire probably has no upward limit; the bird adds new songs and sounds throughout its life.

Birds Bounce, Flap, or Glide

Not all birds fly the same way. Many songbirds use what's called bounding flight: They flap their wings in short bursts to gain altitude, then descend steeply with wings folded against their bodies. The result is a bouncy rhythm in which the bird is constantly climbing and descending, although the overall flight path is level. Bounding flight is perhaps most noticeable in goldfinches, although warblers, orioles, robins, thrushes, and vireos also use it.

Many larger birds use what's called powered flight, in which they constantly flap their wings and so maintain a level course through the air. Flapping and honking Canada Geese use powered flight. Other species undulate—they flap, then glide with their wings held open—or simply glide, as do most hawks.

Hawks Soar on Warm Updrafts

A red-tailed hawk soaring in lazy circles high in the sky is a common sight in many parts of the country. Researchers have learned that soaring birds such as redtails and turkey vultures get a big push from warm air updrafts. As the morning sun rises, it warms the earth's surface, which is not uniform, and so some spots heat up more rapidly. At these locations, the warmer air rises more rapidly than the surrounding air does, forming columns that hawks ride with outstretched wings. These "thermals" can contain vertical gusts of ten miles an hour. Thermals are most common in late morning to midday, making this the best time for soaring birds to be aloft.

During migration, soaring birds rise high on one thermal, then start a long horizontal glide that gradually decreases in altitude until the bird reaches another thermal, which it then uses to rise high once again. Thermals may not form at all in cloudy or rainy weather, and they form later in the day when morning fog keeps the earth cool. Hawk watchers know that in these conditions, opportunities to see soaring birds are limited.

A Dove's Cooing Signals Courtship

The plaintive cooing that gives the mourning dove its name is usually uttered by an unattached male advertising for a mate, though females and mated males occasionally voice this call, too. Males often use favorite perches for calling, but the perch coo does not signify territoriality, since the birds may range and call over a large area.

Migrants arrive back at their place of birth or previous nesting locales in late winter or early spring; from then through summer, courtship and nesting activities are continual. Male doves bow and coo in front of females and perform a flap-glide flight, ending in a long, spiraling glide. The short coo, a briefer version of the perch coo uttered by either sex, often signals selection of a nest site. Perch cooing ceases when a pair bond is formed.

Woodpeckers Make Noise for a Reason

Woodpeckers are unique among birds in that they produce sounds by striking their bills against wood or other materials. These sounds—variously referred to as drumming, tattooing, tapping, and rapping—are used to communicate with members of the same species. Such sounds are also produced when woodpeckers are foraging or excavating nest cavities, but these are incidental sounds that generally play no role in communication.

Downy woodpeckers, common backyard visitors, use a variety of substrates for drumming, from solid or hollow wood to, occasionally, downspouts, gutters, shingles, roofs, and antennae. During a typical drum sequence, downies hit the substrate at a rate of sixteen or seventeen times per second. Drum sequences can vary in duration from about 0.25 second (five hits) to 1.8 seconds (twenty-eight hits).

Downies drum, at varying rates, over a period of about six months, beginning in late winter. Drumming by males serves a variety of functions: establishing and maintaining a breeding territory, attracting and guarding a mate, and stimulating a female. A pair of downies may drum to stay in contact with each other as they forage. In addition to drumming, downies, like other woodpeckers, make a variety of vocalizations to communicate, too.

The Pileated Woodpecker Is a Striking Sight

Bird lovers in areas with old-growth forests are surprised and delighted when an enormous and strikingly patterned woodpecker shows up in the yard. The pileated woodpecker is the country's largest woodpecker—as big as a crow—with a black body, bright red crest, white neckline, and white underwings. Males have a red mustache; females have a black forehead. Because pileated woodpeckers prefer large tracts of land, they are relatively uncommon throughout their range, even though populations seem to have increased in recent years. Some people have had success attracting pileateds to suitably large nest boxes.

The pileated woodpecker is the closest in appearance to the famed ivory-billed woodpecker, the thought-to-be-extinct species that made news in 2005 when a handful of ornithologists and naturalists reported seeing one briefly in an Arkansas swamp. Old films and photos of ivorybills show a bird that's even bigger than the pileated—some twenty inches long—with a pale bill and red, black, and white markings similar to but distinct from the pileated's. Experts who doubt ivorybill sightings suggest that pileated woodpeckers were seen instead.

Cedar Waxwings Share Their Food

Flocks of debonair cedar waxwings are a common sight in trees that hold berries throughout the winter. Waxwings are one of the most frugivorous, or fruit-eating, birds, with a diet that's almost seventy percent fruit. The birds are gregarious; in a flock, they sound their thin, sibilant notes almost constantly. (Their name comes from the bright red patches of color on their wings; the patches look somewhat like old-fashioned letter-sealing wax.) Cedar waxwings aren't migratory but have nomadic habits, with seasonal movements that are sporadic and irregular. They rarely show up in the same place at the same time each year.

The flocks are fun to watch. Waxwings perched on a wire often pass a cherry, flower petal, or caterpillar one to the other all the way down the line. This food passing resembles the bird's courtship display, in which a male and female sidle alongside each other, hopping close, then away, before passing a berry or other food item back and forth until one of the birds eats it. Waxwings are sometimes gluttonous; after gorging on overripe, fermented berries, they may droop and become comically tipsy.

Nuthatches Go Down, Creepers Go Up

The small, chunky white-breasted nuthatch can often be seen zigzagging headfirst down a tree trunk, searching for food in the bark. A foraging nuthatch typically flies from the base of one tree to the top of another, working the trunks from the top down, only occasionally going up the trunk. Unlike woodpeckers, nuthatches don't need stiff, bracing tails for support; their antigravity device is a long, clawlike hind toe on each foot that anchors them to the trees. When feeding on a nut or seed, nuthatches do not hold it with their feet like chickadees or jays. They wedge it tightly in a crevice and hammer it open.

Another small bird that scours tree trunks for food is the brown creeper, but it moves in a different way than the nuthatch does. Brown creepers generally spiral up the tree trunk, starting near the base of a tree and working their way toward the top.

Male Hummingbirds Can Be Bullies

Adult male ruby-throated hummingbirds seem mean-spirited and hot-tempered. When they arrive on their mating grounds in the spring, they are highly charged with hormones, resulting in an obsession with mating and a hair-trigger temper. In fact, a male hummingbird spends just about all of its time in the spring defending the immediate area against other males. From a centralized perch, the bird makes a series of morning vocalizations that mark its territory—usually a repeated *tic-tic*. It moves its head from side to side, scanning for any movement on its turf. The hum of an intruder's wings will agitate it instantly. It will respond with a series of raspy scold calls, perhaps while spreading its tail and fluffing its feathers.

If none of this works, a male rubythroat will fly over to the intruder and make a series of aggressive flights, consisting of rapid, U-shaped dive displays that start as high as forty feet at the top and come to within inches of the offending creature. If all else fails, a hard body slam or feather pull might do the trick. The winner is the bird that doesn't fly away.

Different Hummingbirds Visit Each Day

Hummingbird banders have uncovered some remarkable facts concerning the ruby-throated hummingbird's fall migration. Starting in mid-July, there is almost a complete exchange of birds daily in gardens and at feeders. With few exceptions, during this period, all the birds seen in the yard one day are gone the next, replaced by different birds.

Banders have developed a formula for calculating the number of rubythroats that visit a yard on any given day. They count the largest number of rubythroats seen in the yard at one time, then multiply that figure by five to get a good estimate of how many different birds visit daily. If they see a maximum of six ruby-throats at one time, thirty individuals are actually visiting that day. The numbers visiting a given yard day after day can be astounding. And many millions of others are traveling through the countryside. All of these migrating rubythroats have one goal—to make it across the Gulf of Mexico to reach their tropical winter homes.

Many Birds Won't Visit Feeders At All

No matter how well stocked your backyard bird-feeding station is, you will still attract only a limited number of species. Many types of birds, even ones that are common in your region, never visit backyard feeders, no matter how hungry they are. All wild birds occupy specific niches and so have different requirements for survival. They don't just pick up and move, or change their basic needs, if their requirements aren't met.

Some birds live only in large tracts of woodlands, where they feed, sing, nest, and raise their young. Vireos, ovenbirds, and many warblers are common forest birds that stay away from suburban or fragmented landscapes. Some birds spend most of their lives in the very tops of tall trees; others thrive on the ground, feeding and nesting amid the litter and duff of the woods. Other birds live and feed along bodies of water—unless you live next to a lake, river, or stream, you're unlikely to have waterthrushes, kingfishers, or sandpipers stop by for a visit. Bird lovers recognize the importance of protecting the many and varied environments that different birds depend on to survive.

The Bluebird Represents Ecological Success

During the 1800s, bluebirds were probably about as numerous as robins are today. They were celebrated in story and song—the beloved "bluebird of happiness" was said to carry the sky on its back. But in the middle of the twentieth century, bluebird populations dropped dramatically because of starling competition, a scarcity of nesting cavities, the heavy use of pesticides, and a number of harsh winters. In the past few decades, however, publicity campaigns led by the North American Bluebird Society brought awareness to the bird's plight and inspired direct action to help bluebird populations recover. To that end, bluebird nesting programs, which employed a variety of nest box designs, and bluebird trails, with boxes placed and spaced in good bluebird habitat and regularly monitored by volunteers, headed the recovery efforts.

These projects, along with fortuitously kinder weather and reductions in pesticide use, have paid off, restoring bluebird populations in many areas to levels of stable abundance. From 1966, when breeding surveys began, to 1996, eastern bluebird populations increased by more than one hundred percent. Now more people have a chance to see this favorite species. Almost an entire generation of Americans had missed out on bluebirds in the years when the birds were rare over much of their range.

Crows Seem to Think and Play

Common and well known, if not necessarily well loved, the American crow displays much intelligence and adaptability. A rich anecdotal literature details the bird's cooperative behavior, ability to distinguish subtle cues and clues, and apparent strategies for obtaining food. One observer, for instance, reports that crows drag road-killed animals from the margins into the driving lanes then move away to wait for passing vehicles to macerate the carcasses.

Crows can be taught to mimic human words, and in the wild they sometimes imitate barred owl calls, although most of their vocabulary consists of raucous "aw" and "ah" notes together with a cacophony of bill clacking, growling, and moaning.

One index of crow intelligence is what appears to be creative play behavior. Crows have been seen repeatedly sliding down embankments and the domes of buildings, yanking the tails of mammals, and provoking chases by other birds. Noisy crow mobbing of hawks and owls is a common activity. One noted researcher states emphatically that crows think. Yet, as naturalist

Bil Gilbert cautions, "Crows, like people, cannot be known generally. All descriptions and judgments about them are necessarily limited to what some crows, sometimes, in some places have been known to do."

Common Screech-Owls Are Rarely Seen

Screech-owls are much more abundant than most people realize. Rarely seen during the day, the owl is most often detected by its call (which is more of a tremulous whinny than a screech) during the evening and night. In the daytime, screech-owls roost silently in tree cavities or huddle on branches close to the trunk, resembling bark-colored stubs of the branch itself. They become active after sunset, often hunting prey and feeding throughout the night. On launching from a perch, they drop, then fly straight and low to the ground, rising abruptly to another perch. The flight is completely silent. Along highways, the low-flying habit results in many collisions with cars.

In rural areas, screech-owls favor open woodland and deciduous forest woodlots, often near water. They tend to avoid dense or dry forest habitats. The owls have adapted well to suburban neighborhoods that contain large trees or groves. Parks, cemeteries, and large yards often provide more plentiful food than do rural areas and so have become preferred screech-owl roosting and nesting habitats.

Greater now than they were in presettlement times, screech-owl populations are nonetheless in decline because of urbanization, the loss of fields and hedgerows that house mice, and people's compulsion to "clean up" woodlots by cutting down the snags that are favorite owl nesting sites.

Owls Leave Several Calling Cards

Like hawks and eagles, owls swallow their prey whole, or at least in big chunks. But unlike other birds of prey, owls have relatively weak digestive juices; to get rid of all the indigestible bits of food they swallow, owls regularly regurgitate what are called pellets. These pellets are cylindrical tubes of compressed bones, fur, and feathers formed in the owl's gizzard. After a few hours of digesting and resting, an owl "casts" a pellet (in much the same way as a cat coughs up a fur ball, but not quite as dramatic). It can then go off to find more food—once a pellet is fully formed, an owl can't eat anything.

Pellets are different from droppings. They are often dry and can be found in small piles underneath an owl's favorite roost. Different species leave different sizes of pellets. Smaller owls cast pellets an inch long or less. Larger owls' pellets can be three to four inches long. Scientists who study owls dissect pellets to find out exactly what the birds feed upon.

Another good way to find an owl's roost is to look for whitewash, a layer of accumulated owl excrement, on the trunk of a tree. Just before owls take off, they usually move their bowels, leaving behind another distinct calling card. If a whitewashed tree has pellets underneath it, you've probably found an owl's home.

House Wrens Often Take Over

For its size, the house wren, or "Jenny wren," manifests extremely aggressive behavior toward other birds. To a house wren, almost any other nesting bird in its territory means competition, and so the wren often claims all nest cavities anywhere near its own. If these cavities happen to be occupied by anything smaller than a woodpecker, punctured eggs or dead nestlings are the result. More than a few bluebird lovers have been distressed by the mayhem in their bluebird boxes caused by agitated house wrens. The wrens sometimes attack noncavity nests. House wrens are migratory and have a strong fidelity to their previous breeding territories, so they'll often defend the same space throughout their lives.

For all the pugnaciousness, it's the quality of the male house wren's nesting territory that attracts and keeps a mate. The preferred territory is an open edge area with extended visibility. House wrens are noted for their creative nest sites: They've been known to build nests in tin cans, flowerpots, car radiators, boots, hats, and the pockets of hanging clothes.

Wild Turkeys Are Nothing Like Barnyard Birds

Wild turkeys, which range throughout North America, bear little resemblance to their domesticated brethren, which today are docile, obese, genetically engineered, and mostly reproduced through artificial insemination. By contrast, wild turkeys are streamlined and move surprisingly quickly, and they have a somewhat reptilian appearance.

How the name turkey originated can only be guessed. The likeliest story is that when Cortez brought domesticated Mexican turkeys back to Spain in 1520, people confused them with guinea fowl, which were barnyard birds from the country Turkey. Regardless of their place of origin, descendants of Cortez's birds were soon being raised all over Europe. In fact, the Pilgrim colonists brought farm turkeys with them to America; the four native wild turkeys given to them by their Native American hosts didn't look much different from the ones in their pens.

In colonial America, wild turkeys were so abundant and unwary that hunting them was a chore for children. Naturalist John Madsen once speculated "that the Indians brought turkeys to the Pilgrims' first thanksgiving feast just to get rid of them." Over the years, in this country, turkey replaced goose as the main course at holiday feasts, and turkey quills replaced goose quills as writing instruments. Both the Declaration of Independence and the U.S. Constitution were probably written and signed with turkey feathers.

The Female Oriole Is a Master Builder

The Baltimore oriole's suspended, saclike nest is a durable marvel of tightly woven plant fibers. Usually placed at least thirty feet high at the outermost end of an arched, drooping branch, the nest is difficult to see when trees are in foliage but easy to spot after leaves drop in the fall. American elms were frequent nesting sites before Dutch elm disease killed so many of these trees. Maples, willows, and apple trees are also common sites, but almost any large tree with arching branches may be used.

Nest building, which usually begins in late May, often takes the female Baltimore oriole five to eight days. From a snarl of loose, hanging fibers draped over supporting twigs, the bird goes to work on the dangling strands. Strips of milkweed, dogbane, or Indian hemp bark often provide the tough suspension fibers, along with pieces of string, grapevine bark, and grasses. The oriole feverishly pushes and pulls in shuttlelike movements, randomly weaving from all sides, to create a flexible suspended pouch, open at the top. It lines the chamber with hair, fine grasses, and plant down. Occasionally, an oriole repairs and reuses a nest from the previous spring, but it most often builds a new one each year.

Blame Shakespeare for Starlings

The European starling, one of the most common and, to some, bothersome species of birds, is not native to North America. Starlings were introduced into the United States in 1890 by an amateur ornithologist named Eugene Schieffelin. His idea was to make certain the country was home to every species of bird mentioned in the writings of William Shakespeare (a line from *Henry IV* is "I'll have a starling shall be taught to speak"). Schieffelin released a few cages of imported starlings in New York's Central Park. The birds took to their new home, to say the least—experts estimate the national starling population is now about two hundred million.

Another all-too-common backyard bird, the house sparrow, was also introduced into the United States via release in New York City in the 1800s. In this case, the birds were brought in to reduce the number of caterpillars plaguing the region. Today, the house sparrow thrives just about anywhere people live. Originally known as the English sparrow, the bird isn't a sparrow at all; it belongs to the group of birds known as weavers.

A Sharpie's Diet Is Mainly Other Birds

About ninety-six percent of the sharp-shinned hawk's diet consists of birds, almost any species smaller than itself. An occasionally persistent backyard visitor, the sharpie probably captures more adult passerines—finches, warblers, and other perching birds—than anything else, but it also takes nestlings, rock pigeons, and young chickens in poultry yards (the so-called "chicken hawk" is the slightly larger Cooper's hawk, however).

The sharpie will occasionally eat mice, young rabbits, frogs, and large insects. A common feature of the hawk's near-nest vicinity is a butcher's block or plucking post—a stump, fence post, or other perch where the bird habitually brings its prey, tears it apart, and feeds. Feathers or other prey remnants on the ground may indicate a butcher's block perch and nearby nest.

The sharp-shinned hawk hunts mainly by ambush from inconspicuous woodland perches or by low, gliding flights amid trees and thickets. Unlike the larger buteo hawks, it can quickly maneuver, abruptly turning or dropping when it spots prey. Sharp-shinned hawks sometimes evoke the wrath of bird lovers who believe that hawk attacks on bird feeders are heinous crimes of nature. Sharpies are opportunistic feeders and as such they cull the weak and unwary. Yet they usually avoid human environs unless hunger drives them to bold actions.

Global Warming Has Birds on the Move

Global warming is affecting bird populations, and scientists are working to determine exactly how much. Current research indicates that the ranges of insect-eating birds are likely to be most affected, although a rise in sea level would have a drastic impact on coastal breeding, wintering, and migratory stopover for a variety of species. How quickly will things change? A recent report by the American Bird Conservancy and the National Wildlife Federation cites a pilot study of thirty-five North American warbler species. It found that the range of occurrence of seven of the studied species shifted significantly in the past twenty-five years, by an average of more than sixty-five miles.

States Might Lose Dozens of Familiar Species

The ABC/NWF report predicts what birds will be affected in each state by global warming. In Texas, where birding and bird feeding bring in more than a billion dollars a year, changed summer ranges could well exclude thirty-one species, including the Baltimore oriole, chipping sparrow, and yellow-throated vireo. The summer ranges of another twenty-nine species in Texas, including the Carolina and rock wrens, tufted titmouse, and purple martin, could shrink.

Other states will see similar changes to their summer bird populations, in most cases losing dozens of species, if current projections hold. Virginia would lose the tree and bank swallows, red-breasted nuthatch, and house wren in summer, and the ranges of the gray catbird and American goldfinch would shrink. Maine would lose the boreal chickadee, Nashville warbler, and pine grosbeak; California would lose the black-capped chickadee, red crossbill, and sage thrasher, to name just a few, according to the joint global warming report.

Bird-Watching

Bird-Watchers Need Good Glass

A good pair of binoculars is the first requirement for anyone who wants to take up bird-watching. Good binoculars can make the activity rewarding and enjoyable; a bad pair will make it a pain in the neck. You will probably have to invest at least a hundred dollars for a good pair of birding binoculars—but there are a number of high-quality models at that price (if you want to spend more, of course, you can be sure you'll be able to). To find binoculars for birding, go to a place that sells birding equipment—a nature store or Audubon center—or look at birding magazines to get their advice. Many binoculars, while good at what they do, just aren't made for birding.

You'll notice that every pair of binoculars is labeled with two numbers, something like 7x35 or 10x32. The first number indicates how much a distant object will be enlarged. For example, a 7 means an object will be enlarged seven times. The greater the number, the more powerful the binoculars. The second number refers to the diameter of the objective lens (the big lens) measured in millimeters. The greater this number, the more light the lens lets in, and the brighter the view will be.

Bigger Isn't Necessarily Better

The disadvantage of more powerful binoculars (a 10, say, instead of a 7) is that the image will be susceptible to shakiness if the binoculars are held less than steady. A view through more powerful binoculars will also let you see a smaller patch of sky or tree than less-powerful ones will, and so it will be harder to get your glasses on the bird you want to examine. The disadvantage of bigger lenses is that the binoculars that have them might be too big or heavy to carry comfortably.

Getting the most suitable pair is a trade-off. Many beginning bird-watchers go for 7- or 8-power binoculars of medium size; although if you want to get good looks at distant birds like hawks in flight, a 10 might be the way to go. It's a matter of personal preference. Every expert usually has the same advice about choosing binoculars: You have to try them out and ask many questions to discover which pair will work best for you.

The Right Eye Relief Is Crucial

Bird-watchers who wear eyeglasses need to know about eye relief, which is the optimal distance between a binoculars' eyepieces and the user's eyes. If glasses cause the user to hold the eyepieces farther from the eyes than the binoculars' eye relief, the resulting image will be surrounded by a black ring—it'll be like looking through a hole in a fence. Most glasses-wearing birders need binoculars with an eye relief of at least fourteen millimeters, which manufacturers consider "long" eye relief. The eye relief number should be listed in the binoculars' specifications. Test any model before you buy to make certain the eye relief is right for you. Eye cups, the flexible rings surrounding some binoculars' eyepieces, allow a user without glasses to hold the eyepieces farther away from their eyes if needed to achieve the proper eye relief.

Waterproof Binoculars Make Sense

It makes sense to ensure that your birding binoculars are waterproof, or at least water-resistant. If they are, and if you accidentally drop them in the water, don't throw them away. They're probably still in fine shape. If the water has leaked into products advertised as waterproof or water-resistant, the manufacturer will often fix them for free or offer you a new pair. Even nonwaterproof binoculars that aren't functional after a dunking can usually be made right by a professional, a process that usually isn't all that expensive.

Field Guides Have Photos or Drawings

Another important piece of gear for the bird-watcher is a good field guide. There are a variety of guides available, some aimed at the beginner, some at the expert. A glance at the guides on a bookstore shelf reveals that they usually include either photos of the birds or illustrations. Each type of artwork has its advantages and disadvantages. A photo shows what a certain bird looks like in the wild. It is, obviously, the most realistic depiction possible; and because of this, many beginning bird-watchers prefer guides with photos. But because each individual bird is different, a photo cannot show what a particular species of bird looks like in general. Field-mark details, colors, and feather condition shown in a particular photo are unique to that individual bird. It's difficult, sometimes impossible, to choose one photo that accurately represents a species as a whole.

Illustrations can show in one depiction the field marks and colors that are common to an entire species. And a couple (or quite a few) drawings can show the variety of identifying characteristics many species possess. Because of this, guides with illustrations are the usual choice of more advanced birders. But because the illustrations are idealized, they won't look exactly like any bird you see in the wild. In the end, selecting a field guide is a matter of personal preference. Rest assured that there will always be photos or drawings from which to choose.

Look at the Bird, Not the Guide

One of the great joys of bird-watching is identifying a species you've never seen before. In some cases, putting a name to a new species is easy, but it can often be challenging, especially when a few species look somewhat alike. A good way to improve your identification skills is to practice looking carefully at each bird you see. Take notice of the details of its physical appearance. Is the bill light or dark? What color is the underbelly? Does it have distinctive facial markings? Are the wings plain or striped? Does it have a ring around each eye? To help remember these details, say them to yourself ("reddish crown, gray underneath") or jot them down. Take notice of the bird's behavior, too—how it feeds, moves, and flies.

After you've had a good look at an unfamiliar bird, you can then turn to your field guide to try to find out what it is. But don't spend too much time poring over the pictures and descriptions if the bird is still in front of you. Experts recommend spending more time looking at the bird than looking at the guide. The bird probably won't hang around for long, so you want to get as good a look as you can. And often it's the tiny details of a bird's appearance or behavior that clinches its identity. You'll kick yourself if you missed an important detail because you were looking at the book and not the bird. Spend time studying your field guide when you're not watching the birds so you'll know exactly what to look for when they arrive.

Memorable Phrases Help Identify Singers

Paying attention to birdsong is a great way to increase your appreciation of the birds you see in your yard or the wild. Birders have developed a number of mnemonic devices that will help put names to the songs you hear. In fact, many birds sing their names. The male bobwhite clearly says *bob-white,* the killdeer cries out *killdeer killdeer killdeer,* and the blue jay screams *jay! jay!* Some sing easily remembered nonsense phrases. The red-winged blackbird says *conk-a-reeee.* Common yellowthroats go *witchity-witchity-witchity.* The Amercian bittern says *onk-a-chonk.* The white-breasted nuthatch makes a distinctive *yank yank.*

And some birds sing what seem to be real words (if you have a little imagination). The Carolina wren says *tea kettle, tea kettle, tea kettle;* the eastern towhee suggests that you *drink your tea.* Ovenbirds cry out *teacher, teacher, teacher.* And most guides will tell you that barred owls ask *who cooks for you, who cooks for you all?* Even if you can't identify many birdsongs, if you hear an unfamiliar one, you'll know to look for a great bird nearby.

Planning Helps Backyard Bird Photographers

To take stunning photos of backyard birds it helps to set up a perch on which birds will regularly land. The perch could be on a feeder, or it could be a branch near food or a log with food hidden in holes you've drilled. Carefully positioning the perch is important. Consider the angle of the sun and when you plan to take photos. The perch should not be backlit; ideally, it should be placed so that a nice, even light hits the front of a perched bird. When you've set up a perch, look at it carefully through the camera. Make sure the backdrop is unobtrusive and there are no distracting elements in the frame. If the perch is on a feeder, make sure it will stay steady when a bird perches.

Patience is the key to getting good bird photos. Find a comfortable place to wait—remember that sitting will lower your profile and make you less noticeable to shy birds. Be ready to snap a photo in an instant, because you might not have much more time than a second or two. Film and disk space is relatively cheap, so take as many shots as you can when a good bird arrives. A sturdy tripod with a prefocused camera in place helps enormously. A long lens, in the 200 to 300 range, will allow you to fill the frame with the bird without getting too close.

Serious Birders Keep Life Lists

Some nine hundred different species of birds have been seen in the United States and Canada, and many birders spend lots of time, energy, and money trying to identify as many of these nine hundred birds in the wild as they can. For these dedicated hobbyists, adding to their "life list" is a rewarding pursuit. The longest possible life list is a record of all the species one has seen throughout the world (which is, potentially, ten thousand species), but most North American birders limit their list to Canada and the United States, or just their home country, or their home state or province. Some keep track of the birds seen east of the Mississippi River, or west of it. Some keep a life list just for their county, or their own backyard. Birders have also been known to keep creative lists—the number of different species seen perched on power lines, or at an airport, or spotted from a car.

The World Series of Birding, a fund-raising event held each May in New Jersey, takes listing a few steps further. Participants compete to see which team of birders can positively identify the most species in a twenty-four-hour period. Top World Series teams regularly rack up two hundred species or more.

Volunteers Count Birds for Science

The first Christmas Bird Count was conducted in New York's Central Park in 1900. It was the first attempt to record winter bird populations in the country. Today, some two thousand Christmas Bird Counts are held by bird clubs throughout North America. To conduct a CBC, a group breaks into teams that spend one day between mid-December and mid-January counting birds by species and numbers within a designated area. In many teams, novice birders have the chance to learn from more experienced members. At the end of the day, the teams gather to tally their counts. The U.S. Fish and Wildlife Service is charged with computerizing the counts and making them accessible to researchers. The CBC database constitutes the longest continuous record of bird populations available in North America.

Another annual volunteer bird count is Project FeederWatch, launched in 1987 by the Cornell Laboratory of Ornithology and the Long Point Bird Observatory. It's a continent-wide survey of birds at feeders in private yards. Today, thousands of backyard birders participate in the project, gathering data and submitting it to the lab, which then publishes an analysis of the information it collects.

Birders "Pish" to Get Good Birds

Veteran birders know the only way to get their North American life lists into the three hundred- or four hundred-bird range is to "pish" the more secretive species out of hiding. A birder's pish is a kind of hissing sound with a hard *P* at the beginning made by blowing sharply through the teeth. A pish can also be a smacking sound made by giving the back of two fingers a sharp kiss. Birds may respond to pishing because they think another bird is in trouble, because they think another bird is calling to them, or because they're curious—nobody knows for sure. The goal of pishing is to cause easily excited birds like chickadees and titmice to make a racket so shyer birds that a birder wants to see might come into view for a moment or two.

Birding expert and author Pete Dunne regularly gives pishing workshops for birders who want to master the technique. He's even written a book on the subject. But he admits that a poorly made pish might attract great birds, and a beautiful-sounding pish might do nothing at all.

Playbacks Work but Aren't Always Okay

Another simple way to lure songbirds in for a close look is to play recordings of their songs using a CD player or iPod. But birders should be aware that birds respond to such recordings because they're stressed. When a male bird hears the song of another bird of its species (and sometimes another species), it gets agitated. It often stops whatever it's doing and sings in response or approaches the source of the sound. This is a natural reaction and generally harmless, but playback is best used to lure an already singing bird closer rather than to grab the attention of a silent bird. Attracting birds with playbacks is acceptable in isolated incidents, but it shouldn't happen more than a handful of times to any single bird.

In some cases, however, playback can be genuinely harmful. When rare species attract a lot of birders, or in very popular birding destinations, birds can spend so much time responding to recordings that they neglect vital tasks: finding food, sensing real dangers, caring for their young. To avoid this, some birding hot spots prohibit playback recordings altogether, and birders searching for a rare bird that has attracted or will attract other birders should do so silently.

Good Birds Are Everywhere

Bird lovers who keep their eyes open will discover that many species of birds that don't visit backyard feeders can often be seen within a few blocks or a couple hundred yards of their homes, even if they live in developed areas. Peregrine falcons are now common residents of cities, where they thrive by feasting on rock pigeons. The migration routes of diving ducks, bald eagles, and ospreys often take them near urban areas. Warblers and other songbirds will, on occasion, fill town parks when they "fall out" during migration. Herons breed in suburban neighborhoods that have suitable wetlands.

American kestrels perch on power lines, bobbing their tails while scanning for prey. Red-tailed hawks are commonly visible in trees along highways, or even on light posts and road signs above busy intersections. Chimney swifts and nighthawks twitter and glide through summer city skies. Being alert to the possibility of seeing an interesting bird no matter where you are will add to your enjoyment of bird-watching immensely.

Information in this book was excerpted from *Building a Backyard Bird Habitat*, by Scott Shalaway (2000); *101 Ways to Help Birds*, by Laura Erickson (2006); *Birds of Forest, Yard, and Thicket*, by John Eastman (1997); *Nature-Friendly Garden*, by Marlene A. Condon (2006); *Backyard Birdfeeding*, by John F. Gardner (1996); *Birds of Field and Shore*, by John Eastman (2000); *Bring Back the Birds*, by Russell Greenberg and Jamie Reaser (1995); *Wild Bird Guides: Black-capped Chickadee*, by Susan M. Smith (1997); *Wild Bird Guides: Northern Cardinal*, by Gary Ritchison (1997); *Wild Bird Guides: Ruby-throated Hummingbird*, by Robert Sargent (1999); *Wild Bird Guides: Downy Woodpecker*, by Gary Ritchison (1999); *How Birds Migrate*, by Paul Kerlinger (1995); *The Book of Field and Roadside*, by John Eastman (2003); *Wild Guide: Owls*, by Cynthia Berger (2005); and *Outdoor Safety Handbook*, by Buck Tilton (2006); all published by Stackpole Books.

Additional information was provided by the Cornell Laboratory of Ornithology (www.cornell.birds.edu) and the American Bird Conservancy (www.abcbirds.org).